SUPERMARINE SPITFIRE

IN RAF SERVICE - 1936 TO THE BATTLE OF BRITAIN

MARK POSTLETHWAITE

K5054

Design of the Spitfire began in 1934 as the 'Type 300' and over the next two years was modified to incorporate Air Ministry requirements such as increasing the number of guns from two to eight. When it first appeared in February 1936 it had no guns or undercarriage doors, and bare Alclad panels. The contrast between the various panels is clear on images of the unpainted airframe. Note the original rudder design was very similar to the Me109 rudder. This was soon changed to the more familiar version as seen top right.

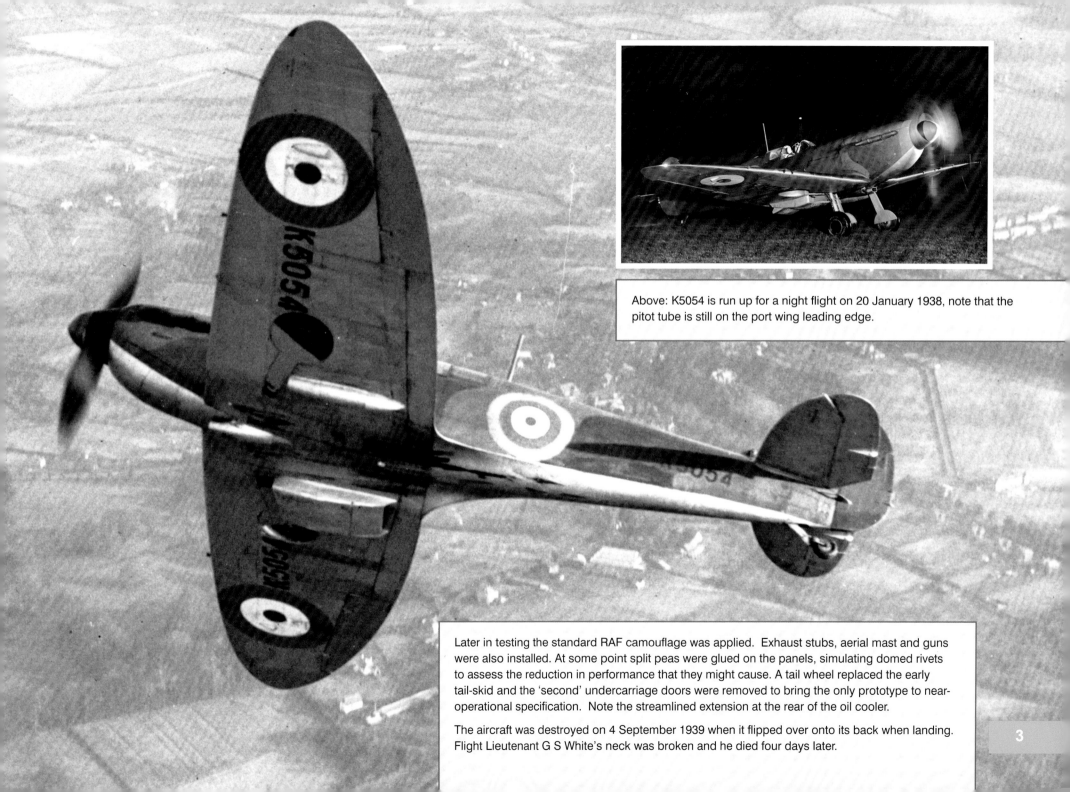

Above: K5054 is run up for a night flight on 20 January 1938, note that the pitot tube is still on the port wing leading edge.

Later in testing the standard RAF camouflage was applied. Exhaust stubs, aerial mast and guns were also installed. At some point split peas were glued on the panels, simulating domed rivets to assess the reduction in performance that they might cause. A tail wheel replaced the early tail-skid and the 'second' undercarriage doors were removed to bring the only prototype to near-operational specification. Note the streamlined extension at the rear of the oil cooler.

The aircraft was destroyed on 4 September 1939 when it flipped over onto its back when landing. Flight Lieutenant G S White's neck was broken and he died four days later.

A Cockpit Guide

- Ring and Bead Gunsight
- Airspeed Indicator
- Artificial Horizon
- Engine RPM Gauge
- Climb & Descent Indicator
- Boost Gauge
- Fuel Pressure Gauge
- Radiator Temp Gauge
- Oil Temp Gauge
- Oil Pressure Gauge
- Turn and Bank Indicator
- Fuel Gauges
- Priming Pump Selector
- Fuel Priming Pump
- Undercarriage Handpump
- Undercarriage Selector
- Fuel Cocks
- Compass Tray
- Rudder Pedals
- Pilot's Seat
- Control Column

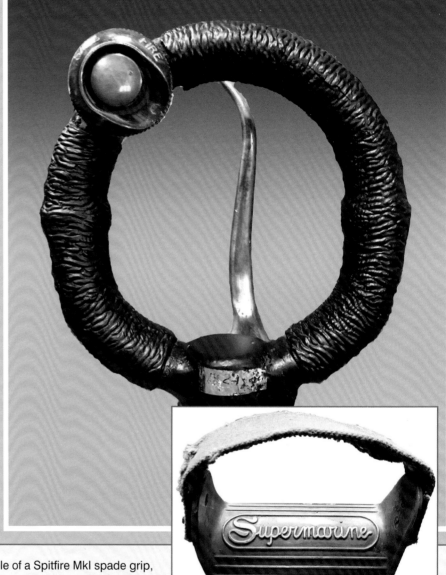

Above: The cockpit of an early K series Spitfire showing the simple ring and bead gunsight and the unarmoured windscreen. The big handle on the right of the cockpit is the undercarriage hand pump which was soon replaced by a less arduous hydraulic system. The reason this handle appears oversized is because it was taken from the Walrus seaplane and literally bent to fit into the Spitfire's snug cockpit!

Above right: A very rare example of a Spitfire MkI spade grip, complete with the red firing button. The spade grip itself was curiously not made of aluminium, (like the Hurricane), but magnesium with just an aluminium gun button knurl, anodised in red. This means that whenever an early Spitfire wreck is excavated, the only thing remaining of the spade grip is the gun button! The silver coloured lever is the brake control.

Right: The early MkI Spitfires were constructed to the highest quality using stainless steel throughout instead of the later carbon steel as production increased. In a very stylish touch, the MkI rudder pedals had the Supermarine logo embossed upon them, again a feature dropped on later marks. Another feature of the early MkIs was the metal seat, this was soon superseded by a moulded composite design.

INTO SERVICE

19 Squadron was the first to be equipped with Spitfires in August 1938. This photo was taken on 31 October 1938. At this time the aircraft had their pre-Munich markings of full yellow/blue/white/red roundels on the fuselage and upper surfaces. The squadron number 19 was apparently painted on the tails shortly before this sortie and removed shortly after. At the time, the Spitfires were being delivered very slowly to the squadron hence why only six aircraft were available for this session.

Note the two different camouflage schemes, the nearest aircraft K9794 has the 'B' scheme and K9797 immediately behind has the 'A' scheme. The original plan of the A and B schemes was that the A scheme would be applied to odd numbered aircraft and the B scheme to even numbered aircraft. This did take place for a while but soon fell by the wayside as production increased.

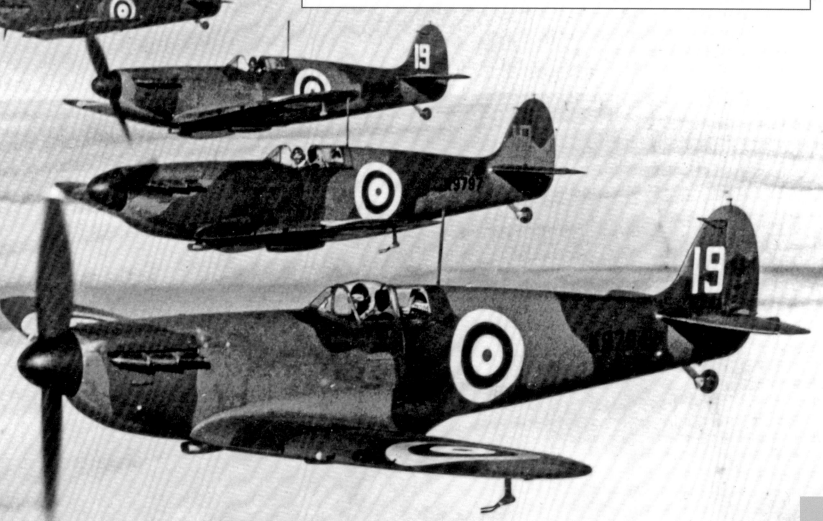

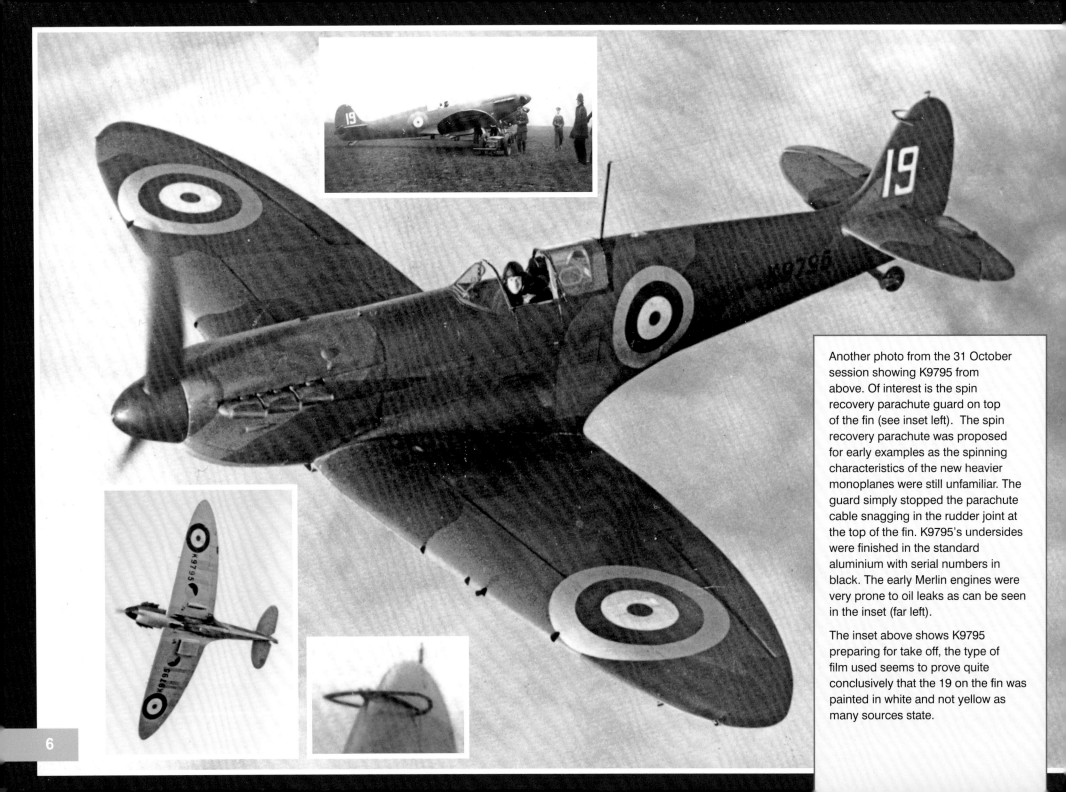

Another photo from the 31 October session showing K9795 from above. Of interest is the spin recovery parachute guard on top of the fin (see inset left). The spin recovery parachute was proposed for early examples as the spinning characteristics of the new heavier monoplanes were still unfamiliar. The guard simply stopped the parachute cable snagging in the rudder joint at the top of the fin. K9795's undersides were finished in the standard aluminium with serial numbers in black. The early Merlin engines were very prone to oil leaks as can be seen in the inset (far left).

The inset above shows K9795 preparing for take off, the type of film used seems to prove quite conclusively that the 19 on the fin was painted in white and not yellow as many sources state.

SPITFIRE K9795 19 SQUADRON, 1938

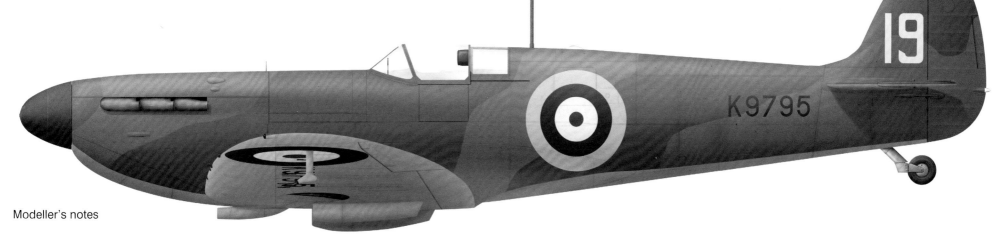

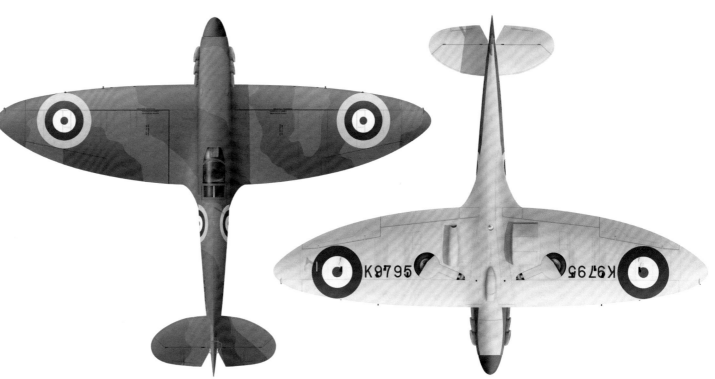

Modeller's notes

Aircraft:

Early pole aerial

Anti spin guard on top of fin

Flat cockpit canopy

No armoured windscreen

Early 2 pronged pitot tube

Ring and bead gunsight

Outer two guns protruding from wing

2 Bladed wooden propeller, blunt spinner

No armour on fuel tank so extra panel lines

No voltage regulator behind pilot's head

Colours:

'A' camouflage scheme

19 in white

Aluminium undersides (no apparent stencilling)

Low demarcation line on nose

Heavy oil staining on undersides.

No red fabric gun patches.

Discussion points:

The underside photo doesn't appear to show any cartridge case ejection holes. These were routinely covered at this time by ground crews using a variety of materials including doped newspaper.

Below: The first operational write-off occurred on 3 November 1938 when Pilot Officer Gordon Sinclair was landing K9792 after his first Spitfire flight at Duxford. The port wheel and axle broke away on landing and the aircraft flipped over. Fortunately Sinclair (inset below) was uninjured. Of interest is the three bladed wooden propeller. 19 Squadron experimented with several different types of propeller during this early period as the big two bladed prop was designed for high-speed and was quite dangerous at low speed.

Left: This Spitfire K9793 was the first to be fitted with a de Havilland three bladed, two pitch propeller. It carried out trials with the A&AEE at Martlesham Heath where it was found to be much safer and delivered better performance than the fixed wooden 2 bladed prop. The DH prop was soon fitted to all Spitfire MkIs on the production line and would eventually be converted to a constant speed unit in time for the Battle of Britain.

Press Day at Duxford on 4 May 1939. By now, all squadrons had been allocated two-letter peacetime codes to be applied to all aircraft. 19 Squadron was allocated WZ for peacetime and QV for wartime. In this photo you can see how the yellow/blue/white/red roundels have been replaced by smaller blue/red versions and the WZ codes have been applied. Serial numbers have also been painted over, (usually reapplied in very smaller digits under the nose or on the fin). Another change not visible is the undersides have been painted with a black port wing and white starboard wing, note the black painted port undercarriage door on the nearest aircraft.

Another view of the line-up on 4 May 1939. Note how the nearest aircraft has a brand new unpainted bulged hood to provide more headroom for the pilot. The second aircraft has the early flat type. The little black tab sticking up from the top of the wing surface is the undercarriage indicator, which when visible, confirmed that the undercarriage was down. None of the aircraft have armoured windscreens yet.

The second aircraft WZ-C is a very early example with the anti-spin guard on the fin and a replacement fuel tank in front of the cockpit. It also has an early external gun camera fitted on the starboard wing root, seen next to the groundcrewman's hand.

A few more photos from the Press Day, In the photo top right, you can see the photographer on a stepladder in the background who took the photo on the previous page. Also noticeable in this photo, (taken with a different filter on the camera), is how light the code letters appear. As the reds of the roundel are very dark, this would suggest that the code letters were painted in a blue/grey which would appear lighter in these circumstances.

The air to air photo on the left just shows that you can't assume anything when it comes to camouflage and markings! WZ-L leading the formation has no overwing roundels and WZ-B leading the second section only has one. This photo also shows that the Spitfires were lined up for the press in sections, so the uncoded one in the foreground of the ground photos is leading C and I at the rear of the formation.

The second squadron to receive the Spitfire was 66 Squadron, also at Duxford. The squadron was allocated RB peacetime codes and LZ wartime codes. Interestingly, and peculiarly to 66 Squadron, RB-V has had the serial number reapplied to the fuselage in light grey paint, the smaller version is still visible on the fin. The light coloured rectangle on top of RB-V's wing root is the early externally mounted camera gun. RB-V was delivered in May 1939 so probably came in the black/white undersides and low vis roundel scheme. Note that this odd numbered aircraft carries the 'B' camouflage pattern, an early deviation from the 'rule'.

Below: RB-A believed to be K9806 was delivered much earlier, in November 1938, and so appears to have had a fair bit of repainting in the fuselage roundel area as the original ones were reduced to just red and blue. The undersides would have been repainted on the squadron from the original aluminium scheme.

SPITFIRE RB-A K9806 66 SQUADRON

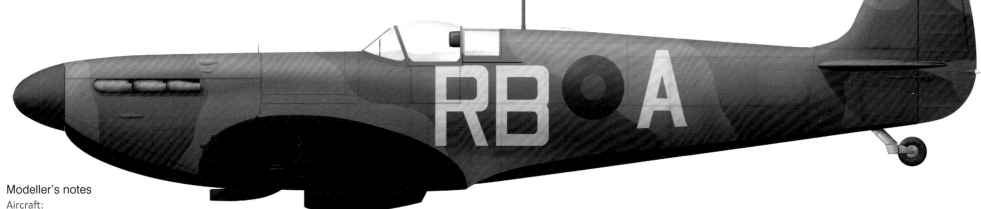

Modeller's notes

Aircraft:

Early pole aerial

Anti spin guard on top of fin

Bulged cockpit canopy

No armoured windscreen

Early 2 pronged pitot tube

Ring and bead gunsight

Outer two guns protruding from wing

2 Bladed wooden propeller, blunt spinner

No armour on fuel tank so extra panel lines

No voltage regulator behind pilot's head

Colours:

'B' camouflage scheme

RB-A in light grey

Black and white undersides, (no stencilling)

Low demarcation line on nose

Heavy oil staining on undersides.

No red fabric gun patches.

Serial possibly stencilled on fin

Reduced size upper wing roundels

Discussion points:

The black and white undersides are assumed
based upon the fuselage underside looking
white rather than aluminium.

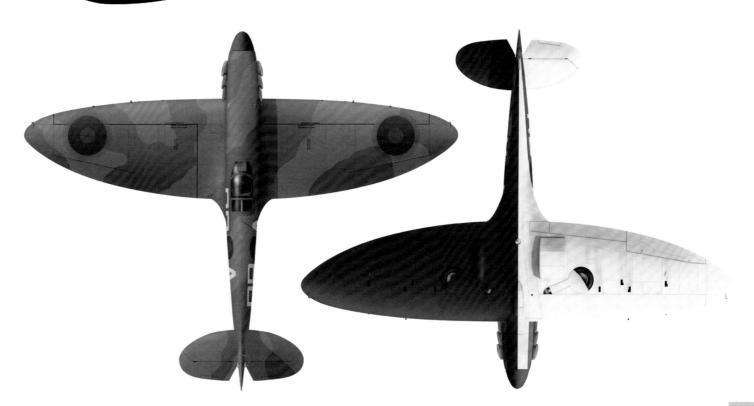

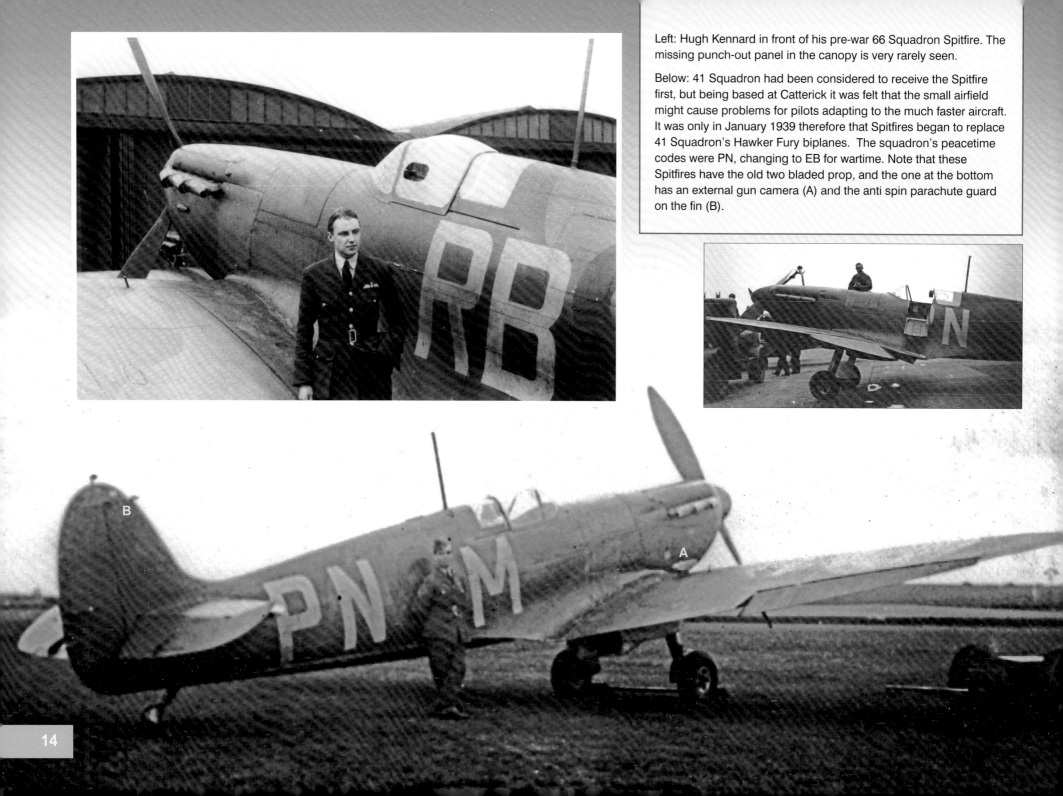

Left: Hugh Kennard in front of his pre-war 66 Squadron Spitfire. The missing punch-out panel in the canopy is very rarely seen.

Below: 41 Squadron had been considered to receive the Spitfire first, but being based at Catterick it was felt that the small airfield might cause problems for pilots adapting to the much faster aircraft. It was only in January 1939 therefore that Spitfires began to replace 41 Squadron's Hawker Fury biplanes. The squadron's peacetime codes were PN, changing to EB for wartime. Note that these Spitfires have the old two bladed prop, and the one at the bottom has an external gun camera (A) and the anti spin parachute guard on the fin (B).

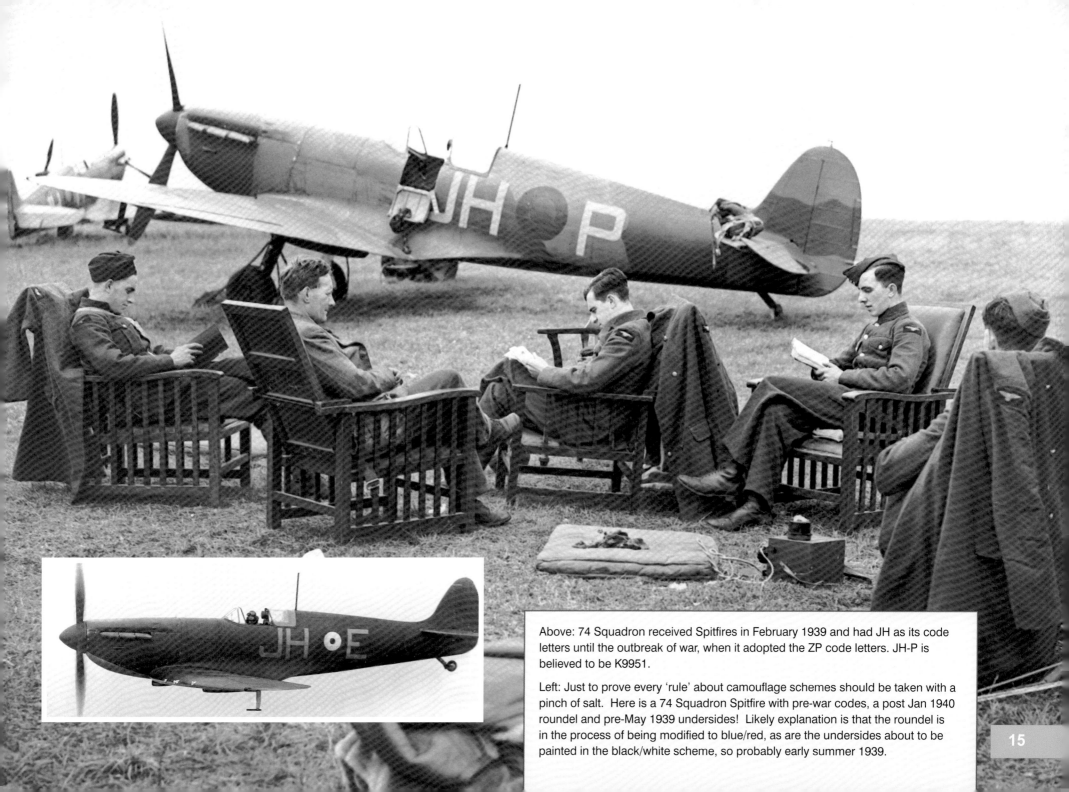

Above: 74 Squadron received Spitfires in February 1939 and had JH as its code letters until the outbreak of war, when it adopted the ZP code letters. JH-P is believed to be K9951.

Left: Just to prove every 'rule' about camouflage schemes should be taken with a pinch of salt. Here is a 74 Squadron Spitfire with pre-war codes, a post Jan 1940 roundel and pre-May 1939 undersides! Likely explanation is that the roundel is in the process of being modified to blue/red, as are the undersides about to be painted in the black/white scheme, so probably early summer 1939.

65 Squadron received Spitfires in March 1939, applying its peacetime codes of FZ to the fuselages upon delivery. This photo is believed to have been taken shortly after their arrival at Hornchurch. It is interesting to note that some aircraft already have the black and white undersides, (probably applied in the factory) whereas the nearest Spitfire K9912, still has the original aluminium paint. K9912 will appear quite a few times in this book!

This selection of photos all show 65 Squadron Spitfires in spring/summer 1939. FZ-P (below) has the external camera gun fitted (arrowed). In a lot of the pre-war air to air photos of Spitfires, the pilots have the cockpit hoods open. This is not unusual as the headroom was very tight, even with the bulged canopy, and most pilots had been flying open cockpit biplanes before converting to Spitfires. K9912 from the previous page is FZ-O in the formation on the right.

54 Squadron received Spitfires in March 1939 at Hornchurch, replacing its biplane Gladiators. Peacetime codes were DL changing to KL in September 1939. Note the squadron emblem on the fin.

Above: 602 Squadron received its Spitfires in May 1939 and applied its peacetime codes of ZT to them. At the outbreak of war the squadron's codes changed to LO. Note the very small roundel which was also seen on the upper wings of older 602 Sqn aircraft well into 1940, like this early build Spitfire pictured (right) in June 1940.

72 Squadron received Spitfires in April 1939 at Church Fenton. The groundcrew also applied the squadron crest to the tail fin as can be seen here on SD-H K9938. The peacetime SD codes were replaced by RN at the outbreak of war. Interestingly, another photo of this aircraft (left) shows that it wears no upper wing roundels at all.

611 Squadron received its Spitfires in May 1939. Here the mayor of Liverpool is shown around this brand new fighter at Speke (now Liverpool airport). 611 was allocated the peacetime code of GZ, changing to FY on the outbreak of war. Note how this aircraft also has an upperwing roundel much smaller than typical Battle of Britain period roundels. This was a result of the conversion of the large yellow/blue/white/red down to just two colours, blue/red painted over the centre of the old roundel.

HAND TURNING GEAR
FOR MAINTENANCE ONLY
IF USED FOR EMERGENCY STARTING
AIRCRAFTSMAN MUST HAVE ROPE FROM
HIS WAIST TO THE UNDERCARRIAGE
TO PREVENT HIM FALLING INTO THE
AIRSCREW.

Note the protruding blast suppressors on the outer machine guns, typical of early Spitfires. These blast suppressors were soon removed in service to allow the gun ports to be taped over to keep the guns warm and also to keep dirt out of the gun muzzles. The black hole with the metal plate underneath just above the leading edge wing root is the hand cranking point for turning the engine manually (see inset). This is the biggest recognition feature of the MkI against the MkII which had this removed.

THE SPEED SPITFIRE

In late 1937, a Spitfire was taken off the production line to be modified in an attempt to break the landplane speed record. K9834 was extensively modified with a four bladed wooden prop, enlarged radiator and oil cooler, streamlined canopy as well as an uprated engine and fuel systems. The highly polished blue and silver N.17 achieved 408mph in February 1939 but was constantly behind the Germans as they pushed the record to over 450mph just a month later. With war clouds looming, the project was shelved and K9834 was modified back to a PR MkII but kept its distinctive lightning flash on the fuselage.

WAR!

609 Squadron received its Spitfires in August 1939, so hardly had time to apply its peacetime codes of BL before going onto a war footing with PR codes.

The inset photo shows a very rare combination of wartime codes with the blue/red fuselage roundel which only lasted for a couple of months before the blue/white/red roundel was introduced on the fuselage sides. At around the same time, armoured windscreens were being installed externally to all Spitfires, as can be seen in the larger photo.

When war was declared, squadrons were required to change their codes from the peacetime list to the wartime list. For 65 Squadron this meant replacing its FZ codes with YT. This Spitfire K9906, seen above being flown by Robert Stanford-Tuck, had its YT codes applied in rather a hurry by the looks of it! The brown paint used to cover the FZ codes has obliterated some of the fuselage roundel and the new 'T' is not exactly on the same angle as the 'Y'. As 65 Squadron's codes were usually pretty smart, it's possible that this photograph was taken just after war was declared and the 'temporary' markings were subsequently improved. Note the serial number is still just visible on the fuselage and is also painted on the fin.

THE EVOLUTION OF MARKINGS

When N3035 was delivered to 66 Squadron in October 1939 the official markings were black and white undersides with toned down national markings of just red and blue roundels. The serial number was also removed from its usual position on the fuselage and may have been applied in small numerals on the tail fin.

The 66 Squadron groundcrew applied the unit's LZ codes and individual letter K on either side of the roundel and were one of the few squadrons to re-apply the serial on the fuselage, although uniquely in grey paint.

Just a month or so later, an order was received to add a white ring to the fuselage roundel to aid identification after a series of 'friendly fire' incidents. The groundcrew clearly didn't want to repaint the codes so just enlarged the roundel to slightly overlap the letters.

In May 1940 with the invasion of France, the Spitfire squadrons were sent to patrol the skies over Dunkirk and quickly needed far more visible markings in the hectic combats that were taking place. Roundels were added under the wings, a fin flash applied to the tail and a yellow outer ring applied to the fuselage roundel. With the urgency of the situation, the groundcrew must have assumed that the markings were more important than the code letters and so further obliterated them.

With the action over Dunkirk dying down, the pilots were not happy with their very visible black and white undersides, and so orders were sent out to repaint all undersides of RAF fighters in 'Sky', which was interpreted in many different shades by squadrons due to the lack of official supplies of the colour.

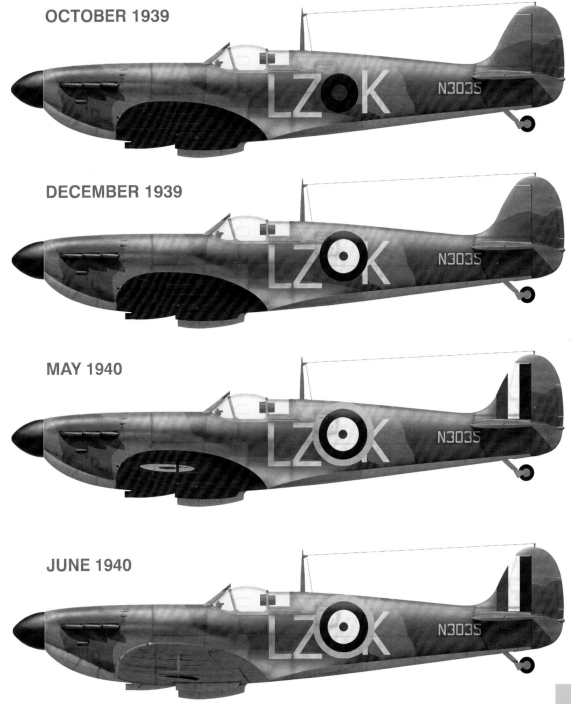

OCTOBER 1939

DECEMBER 1939

MAY 1940

JUNE 1940

Right: A nice air to air of a 609 Squadron Spitfire PR-B in early 1940. Note the '100' stencilled on the fuel tank reminding ground crews to use the new 100 octane fuel which gave the Spitfire better performance.

Below: Another view of PR-O seen on the opening page in this section with a cartoon dog(?) nose art (inset). The thick armoured windscreen is very clear in this view.

Bottom right: Another example of 609 Squadron Spitfire nose-art, this one being a hare saying 'pah'.

Background photo: With the outbreak of war, 611 Squadron changed its codes to FY and later moved to Digby in Lincolnshire where this photo was taken. K9999 was later transferred to 152 Squadron and was shot down into the sea off the Isle of Wight on 12th August, its pilot Pilot Officer Douglas Shepley was killed but his body never found.

Inset top left: 72 Squadron also changed its codes, from SD to RN, as seen on this early K series Spitfire, note the early 'ring pull' door locking mechanism.

Inset left: 19 Squadron at Duxford changed it's codes from WZ to QV as the winter of 1939 set in.

Inset top right: 66 Squadron, also at Duxford, changed its codes from RB to LZ but still couldn't make up its mind what colour to paint the serials! Here is N3040 with a grey serial and N3121 with the standard black lettering at Duxford in early 1940.

GAS PATCHES

A noticeable feature of a number of Spitfire MkIs was a square or diamond shaped patch, usually seen on the port wing. This was a gas detection patch which changed colour in the presence of poisonous gas.

It is fair to assume that they were introduced shortly after the outbreak of war, being very easy to apply, either as a fabric patch or directly using special paint. They were light yellow/green in colour and if patched, would have dark/red tape around the edges. The most popular position is as seen in the photo of a 602 Sqn Spitfire top right. The main factor was of course for it to be in a position away from any removable panel. Smaller versions were also seen in front of the aileron as seen in the two images near right.

As the fear of a gas attack faded, so did the presence of the patches and they were rarely seen on Spitfires from September 1940 onwards although there were exceptions even into 1941.

A new 64 Squadron Spitfire is wheeled into a hangar. The squadron didn't receive Spitfires until April 1940 so this photo must have been taken around that time as in May 1940, fin flashes and a yellow ring around the fuselage roundel were introduced. Note the unpainted sliding canopy, presumably a replacement for the originally fitted flat version.

Inset: EB-M of 41 Squadron also with a replacement canopy

Three 65 Squadron Spitfires lined up in a newly constructed blast-pen in early 1940. K9911 has a very small gas detection patch on the starboard wing and small overwing roundels. It also has a plate fitted on the armoured fuel tank to attach a shield to hide the pilot's eyes from exhaust glare when flying at night. The stencil next to the hand cranking plate reads '12 Volt Starting Only'. In the middle is K9907 YT-D which was shot down on 8 July 1940.

At the rear is L1094 YT-H. The rear two aircraft have the serial painted on the fin whereas K9911 shows evidence of it being painted out. Note that all three Spitfires go against the 'rule' of 'A' Scheme for odd serials and 'B' Scheme for even serials.

SPITFIRE K9911 YT-E 65 SQUADRON

Modeller's notes

Aircraft:
Early pole aerial
Bulged cockpit canopy
Armoured windscreen
Mount for night vision exhaust shield
Standard pitot tube
Reflector gunsight but with bead mount on cowling
Red patches on guns
DH 3 bladed propeller
No voltage regulator behind pilot's head

Colours:
'B' camouflage scheme
YT-E in light grey
Black and white undersides, (no stencilling)
Low demarcation line on nose
Reduced size upper wing roundels
Yellow gas detection patch on starboard wing

Discussion points:
This aircraft shows signs of being repainted as the
pattern on the port wing and fuel tank are non standard.
The small gas patch may have been repeated on the port
wing as seen on several other aircraft.

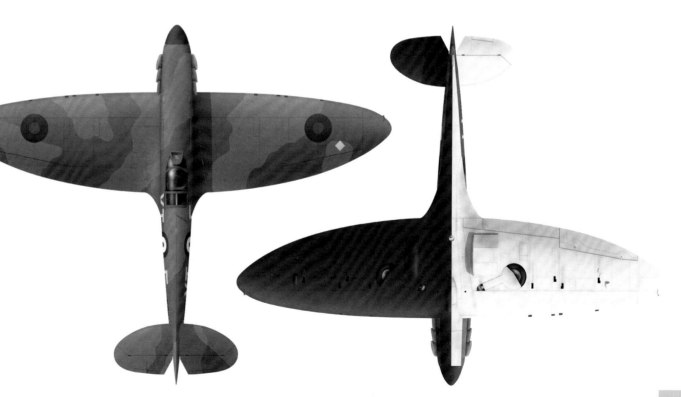

PROTECTING THE PILOT

As soon as war broke out, it was noted that the Spitfire provided very little protection for its pilot. Dowding, the Commander in Chief of RAF Fighter Command, was very insistent that armour be added to his Spitfires and Hurricanes, despite the official view that they were so fast that nothing could shoot at them from behind!

First came a thin sheet of metal over the fuel tank designed to deflect bullets fired at an angle. Then came the armoured windscreen, shortly followed by the 6.5mm thick head armour which was mounted behind the pilot's headrest. The final piece of armour for the pilot came in the form of a 4.5mm thick sheet of metal that was inserted behind the pilot's seat.

Possibly the shortest pilot ever to sit in a Spitfire! The seat armour can be seen in the foreground. The cut out corners were to allow the plate to fit around equipment.

King George VI inspecting an early Spitfire, note the basic framework behind the pilot's seat without any armour.

Sunlight catches both seat and head armour in this Battle of Britain Spitfire.

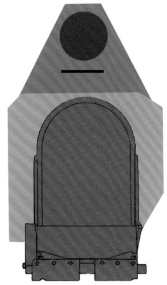

A diagram showing the head armour (blue) which was placed behind the seat armour (green).

Above: Hugh Kennard in his 610 Squadron Spitfire showing the newly installed armoured windscreen, note that it isn't as tall as the original windscreen frame. This armoured glass undoubtedly saved lives, the damage to the windscreen (right) was sustained during a head on attack.

Top right: The standard Spitfire MkI canopy was bulged on top but still flat sided, the commonly known Spitfire canopy which was also bulged at the sides only appeared in October 1941. The rectangular rounded object in the port side of the canopy was a panel that could be punched out in an emergency to help equalise the pressure inside and out. This would help open the canopy in the same way as releasing the pressure in a jam jar makes it easier to unscrew the lid. This photo shows Leonard Haines in the cockpit of his 19 Squadron Spitfire.

Right: Combat experience soon showed that a rear view mirror was desperately needed. The mirror was not for clear study of the Spitfire's tail but more for a suggestion of movement behind the aircraft which would be enough to alert the pilot to 'check six'. Without the mirror, the pilot would constantly be having to turn his neck, which in combat could be extremely uncomfortable. This 610 Squadron Spitfire has a mirror fitted internally by the ground crew. Externally fitted mirrors were soon to be more common and eventually were fitted at the factory as standard.

The reflector gunsight can be seen. During the Battle of Britain the glass was always circular, the square version coming into service after the Battle.

In May 1940, markings were again changed as pilots still found difficulty in identifying friend or foe in the increasing number of combats now taking place. An order was sent out to all fighter squadrons to add a yellow outer ring to the fuselage roundel and to paint a red/white/blue fin flash on the fin.

The photo on the left is rare because it shows a 72 Squadron Spitfire with a fin flash but not the yellow surround to the roundel, which must be next on the list for the groundcrew.

Below is another rare photo of fin flashes being applied to newly delivered Spitfires at Tangmere in May 1940. These R66 series aircraft were delivered to 238 Squadron on its reformation there and given the codes VK. Within a month however, the Spitfires were taken from 238 and sent to front line squadrons as the action over Dunkirk intensified.

238 Squadron had Spitfires for less than a month before being requipped with Hurricanes for the Battle of Britain. The photos below therefore are incredibly rare, showing VK coded Spitfires at Tangmere, the undersides would still be in the black/white scheme.

The Spitfires were brand new and were serialled from R6599 to R6613. Most of them subsequently went to front line squadrons and fought in the Battle of Britain.

The aircraft landing in the background is an Armstrong Whitworth Ensign used for moving squadron personnel between bases.

Left: Spitfires coming out of the factory after war was declared were finished in the standard Fighter Command underside scheme of black port wing and white starboard wing. The remainder of the undersides were aluminium. These newer aircraft are easily identified by having the white stencilling on the black wing. When the black wing was added to the early K and L series aircraft, the groundcrews simply painted over the stencilling. This Spitfire P9450 first flew on 5 April 1940.

THE EVOLUTION OF THE MkI SPITFIRE

The MkI Spitfire received dozens of modifications during its production life, some more visible than others. These two photos show an early K series Spitfire alongside one of the last R series MkIs.

double pronged pitot tube on very early models only

early ring and bead gunsight

although bulged on this example, the very early MkIs had flat canopies

unarmoured fuel tank note the extra panel lines subsequently hidden by the armour plate

early pole aerial mast

K9912

Early K series door locking mechanism (left) had a metal ring between two wires.

Later MkIs had a handle and bolt mechanism (right).

K9912 also appears elsewhere in this book and ended up burnt out on a beach near Dunkirk, see pages 16, 17 and 37.

34

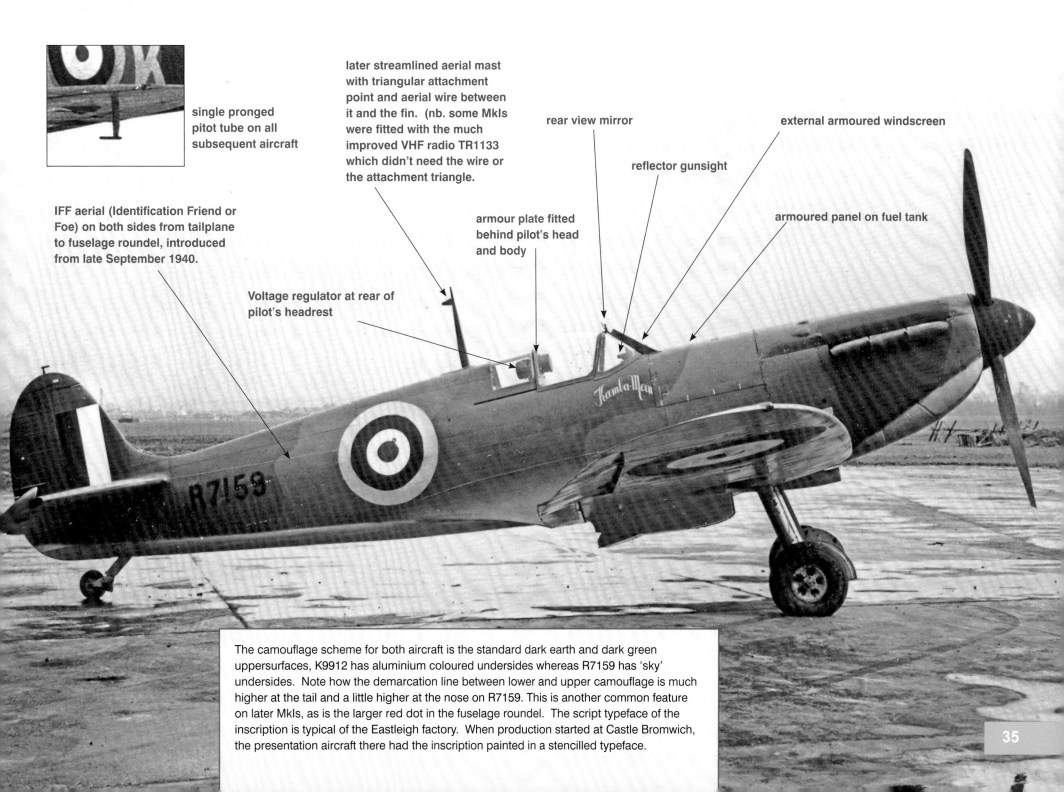

single pronged pitot tube on all subsequent aircraft

later streamlined aerial mast with triangular attachment point and aerial wire between it and the fin. (nb. some MkIs were fitted with the much improved VHF radio TR1133 which didn't need the wire or the attachment triangle.

rear view mirror

external armoured windscreen

reflector gunsight

IFF aerial (Identification Friend or Foe) on both sides from tailplane to fuselage roundel, introduced from late September 1940.

armour plate fitted behind pilot's head and body

armoured panel on fuel tank

Voltage regulator at rear of pilot's headrest

The camouflage scheme for both aircraft is the standard dark earth and dark green uppersurfaces, K9912 has aluminium coloured undersides whereas R7159 has 'sky' undersides. Note how the demarcation line between lower and upper camouflage is much higher at the tail and a little higher at the nose on R7159. This is another common feature on later MkIs, as is the larger red dot in the fuselage roundel. The script typeface of the inscription is typical of the Eastleigh factory. When production started at Castle Bromwich, the presentation aircraft there had the inscription painted in a stencilled typeface.

A sorry looking K9956 XT-P of 603 Squadron which overshot on landing at Drem in a heavy rainstorm and overturned at 17.35 hrs, 17 April 1940. Plt Off W A Douglas was uninjured. Note the Spitfire has 'Eboracum' painted on both sides of the nose (the Roman name for York).

The inside of the flaps is rarely seen in photos as they were nearly always retracted when parked.

K9912, (seen in earlier photos in this book), was delivered to 65 Squadron in March 1939 and later wore the code letters YT-O. It was force-landed on the beach near Dunkirk on 26 May 1940 by 18-year-old Pilot Officer Kenneth Hart who set fire to the aircraft. Ken Hart (below) was evacuated from Dunkirk two days later.

Left: N3180 KL-B was named 'Kiwi' by its pilot, New Zealand Ace Alan 'Al' Deere.

On 23 May 1940 he was shot down in KL-B over Dunkirk and force-landed on the beach (below). The aircraft caught fire and 'Al' Deere was dragged unconscious from the cockpit by a soldier. Deere was evacuated and continued his legendary career in various other 'Kiwi' Spitfires. Note that this Spitfire has a Rotol prop and spinner and no aerial wire from the mast.

Right: In November 1939, 54 Squadron was selected to test a new improved Spitfire. The 22 new aircraft, delivered the following month, were fitted with constant speed Rotol metal propellers and the much improved VHF radio TR 1133 which didn't need an aerial wire between the mast and the tail. The Rotol prop was easily identified by a larger blunt spinner as can be seen in these photos.

The constant speed propeller is a little like an automatic gearbox in a car. The propeller constantly adjusts its pitch to best suit the power inputs of the pilot. The previous 'variable pitch' propellers had to be adjusted by the pilot for various stages of flight.

SPITFIRE N3180 KL-B 54 SQUADRON

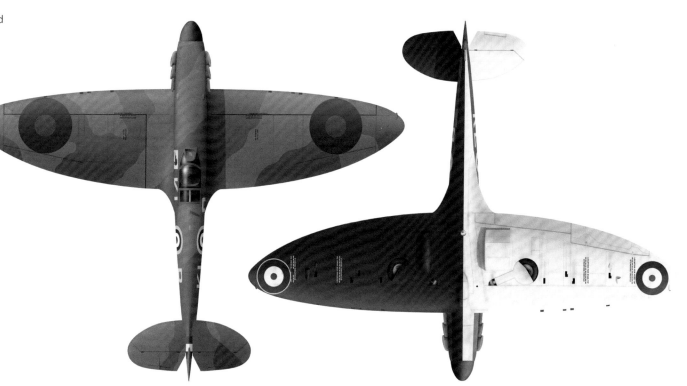

Modeller's notes

Aircraft:
Later aerial mast but with no triangle attachment point and
no aerial wire
Bulged cockpit canopy
Armoured windscreen
Standard pitot tube
Reflector gunsight
Rotol propeller and blunt spinner
Armoured fuel tank

Colours:
'B' camouflage scheme
KL-B in grey
Black and white undersides, (with stencilling)
Low demarcation line on nose
No serial

Discussion points:
Aircraft delivered in Jan 1940 so probably had low vis
red/blue roundels on fuselage, modified to non standard
roundel subsequently. As undersides were delivered in
black and white scheme, stencilling would probably still be
there. Upperwing roundels were probably full sized but
difficult to see on main photo. Also gas detection patches
might have been carried on both wings, similar to the
aircraft on the next page.

Main photo and top right: This Spitfire landed wheels down on the beach near Dunkirk and has never been positively identified. However, the Rotol propeller would strongly suggest 54 Squadron and the only likely candidate for that would be N3103 which was force landed by George Gribble on 25 May 1940. Apparently Gribble himself removed the new TR1133 radio and others removed ammunition boxes before setting the aircraft on fire. This would explain why all hatches are open. Of interest from a markings point of view are the two small gas detection patches, one on each wing applied on top of the roundels.

Left insets: Two 74 Squadron ZP coded Spitfires that were captured during the Battle of France. Top left is probably K9977 which was force-landed at Berck-sur-Mer on 21 May by its pilot P/O R D Aubert. Left is K9867 ZP-J flown by S/Ldr Frank L White which force-landed at Calais-Marck on 23 May 1940.

Below: A detailed close-up of what is believed to be Flying Officer Ian Russell of 609 Squadron who was lost when shot down off Dunkirk in L1058 on 1 June 1940. His aircraft has the old style pole aerial but does have the armoured windscreen, armoured fuel tank and head armour behind the headrest.

Left: A 609 Squadron Spitfire at Northolt during the Dunkirk evacuation period. This is an early K series Spitfire with the original door mechanism and reduced upper-wing roundels. Note the small outboard gas patch, again maybe carried on the starboard wing as well.

This Spitfire is believed by some historians to be a 222 Squadron Spitfire on the beach near Dunkirk although the spinner does look like another 54 Squadron Rotol. Events of that period were so confused and many records were lost, so it's difficult to be certain.

There are many interesting points to note. Firstly the aileron, being fabric covered, has burnt back to the ribs whilst the metal skinned wing remains intact.

Secondly, this aircraft was clearly delivered in the black and white undersides scheme as the white stencilling is still in place. (When ground crews painted over the original aluminium undersides on early aircraft they simply painted over these stencils). This Spitfire also has the black/white scheme on the nose and presumably the fuselage as well.

Note the position of the 'Location for wing tip steadying trestle' stencil. It might sound obvious but these stencils MUST line up with the aileron tabs as that's where the strong point was. Many modellers and profile artists place these randomly to fit with everything else!

The roundel has been painted on the squadron, note the brush strokes in the white. It was probably blue/white/red first with the yellow being added at a later date judging by how the thin yellow outer encroaches on the stencilling. The yellow outline wasn't official until after Dunkirk but it was unofficially added by many squadrons.

THE BATTLE OF BRITAIN

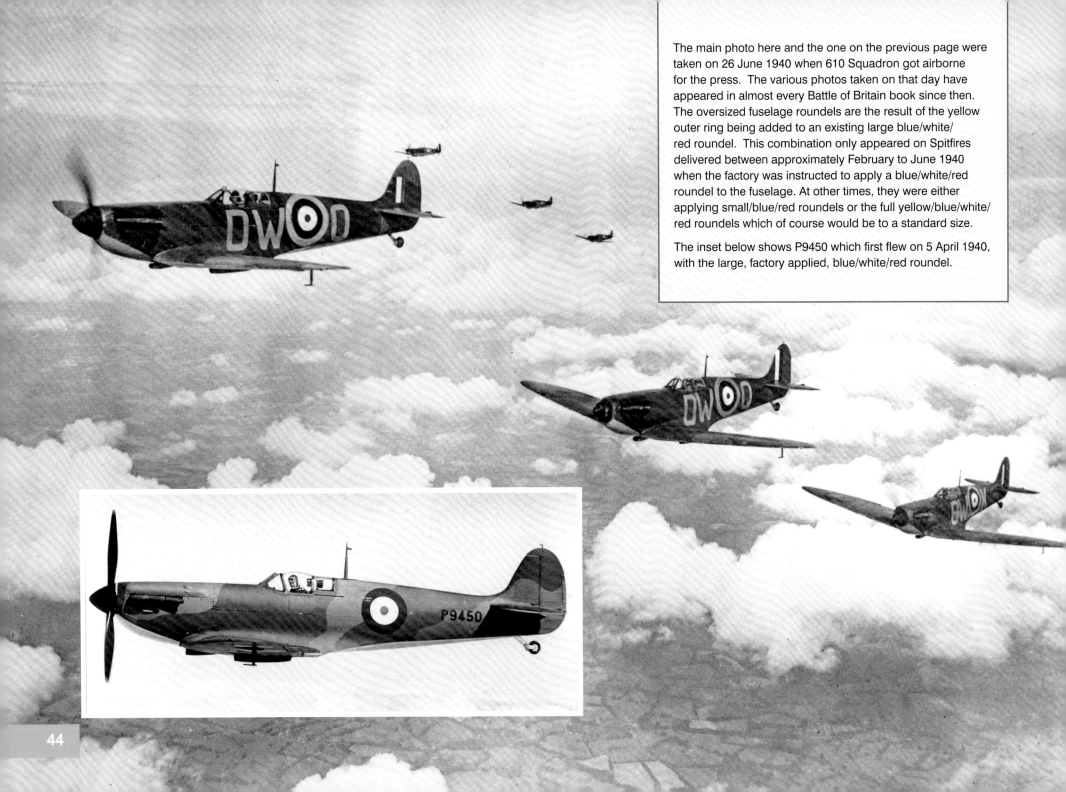

The main photo here and the one on the previous page were taken on 26 June 1940 when 610 Squadron got airborne for the press. The various photos taken on that day have appeared in almost every Battle of Britain book since then. The oversized fuselage roundels are the result of the yellow outer ring being added to an existing large blue/white/red roundel. This combination only appeared on Spitfires delivered between approximately February to June 1940 when the factory was instructed to apply a blue/white/red roundel to the fuselage. At other times, they were either applying small/blue/red roundels or the full yellow/blue/white/red roundels which of course would be to a standard size.

The inset below shows P9450 which first flew on 5 April 1940, with the large, factory applied, blue/white/red roundel.

Sergeant Claude Parsons of 610 Squadron has his radio set inspected by an entire team of groundcrew, all keen to get into the press photo at Hawkinge on 29 July 1940. Although the Spitfire MkI was mainly constructed of metal, the control surfaces were all fabric covered. The rectangular section on the back of the elevator is the trim tab. This feature allows the pilot to trim the aircraft at different power settings so that the aircraft flies 'hands off' without needing constant forward or backward pressure on the control column.

Note that 610 Squadron was one of the first to fit rear view mirrors to its Spitfires, this one being mounted externally.

There were no official instructions as to the size that the fin flash should be painted so DW-D got a full height version, DW-K got an almost full sized one and DW-O got the shortest of all and possibly with its colours reversed! The undersides of all aircraft at this point should have been sky overall with no underwing roundels.

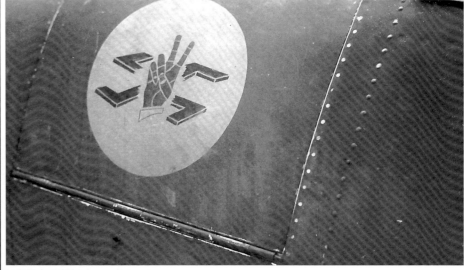

Above: N3277 AZ-H of 234 Squadron in a field near Cherbourg on 15 August 1940. An order had gone out on 11 August to repaint roundels underneath the wings but clearly this hadn't been completed by the squadron 4 days later.

Below: The Germans were quick to hide their 'prize'.

Above: The unofficial emblem carried by many 234 Squadron Spitfires during the Battle of Britain and beyond.

Below: Many sources state that the damage behind the cockpit was due to the pilot detonating the IFF equipment destruction charge. However, the IFF equipment wasn't carried at this time and the inset photo clearly shows a 20mm cannon shell entry hole on the port side.

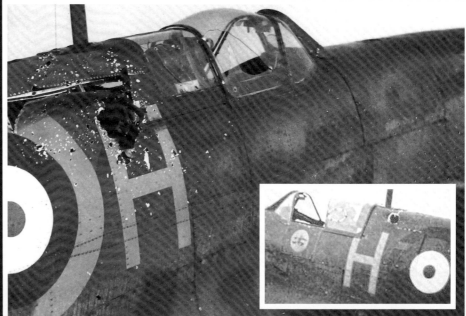

SPITFIRE N3277 AZ-H 234 SQUADRON

Modeller's notes

Aircraft:
Standard aerial
Bulged cockpit canopy
Armoured windscreen
Standard pitot tube
Reflector gunsight
Standard DH prop and spinner
Internal rear view mirror

Colours:
'A' camouflage scheme
AZ-H in light grey
Sky undersides, (no stencilling)
Low demarcation line on nose
Red fabric gun patches.
234 Squadron unofficial emblem on door
'Dirty Dick' written on both sides of fuel tank.

Discussion points:
Note the cut out to the fuselage roundel's yellow outer ring. This is probably to show the stencilling on the radio compartment door as the aircraft was delivered with just a blue/white/red roundel.
The unofficial emblem has always been assumed to be yellow, but the inset photo on the opposite page, taken with orthochromatic film, shows a huge difference between the yellow of the roundel and the emblem. We've therefore chosen a pale blue for the profile, but this is not confirmed.

CAPTURED SPITFIRES

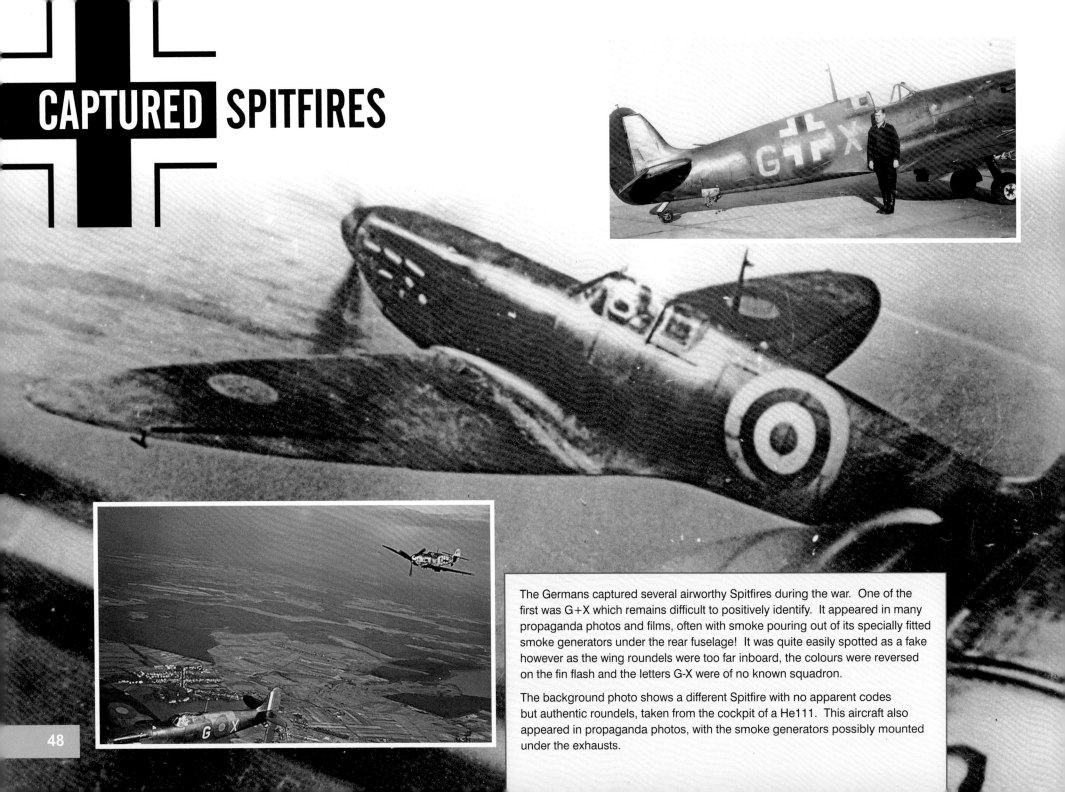

The Germans captured several airworthy Spitfires during the war. One of the first was G+X which remains difficult to positively identify. It appeared in many propaganda photos and films, often with smoke pouring out of its specially fitted smoke generators under the rear fuselage! It was quite easily spotted as a fake however as the wing roundels were too far inboard, the colours were reversed on the fin flash and the letters G-X were of no known squadron.

The background photo shows a different Spitfire with no apparent codes but authentic roundels, taken from the cockpit of a He111. This aircraft also appeared in propaganda photos, with the smoke generators possibly mounted under the exhausts.

Right and right inset: In addition to AZ-H, another Spitfire that force landed in France on 15 August was K9964 SH-W of 64 Squadron, flown by F/O Ralph Roberts. The photos shows it shortly after force-landing in a field and then back on its undercarriage.

Below and left inset: Later on in the Battle, on 6 September 1940, Pilot Officer James Caistor force-landed his factory fresh 603 Squadron Spitfire X4260 XT-D near Calais.

Armourers rearm Spitfire R6800 LZ-N the personal aircraft of 66 Squadron's CO, Squadron Leader Rupert Leigh at Gravesend, September 1940. The men are loading full ammunition boxes into the hatches. One armourer would then go on top of the wing (inset) to thread the belts through the machine guns before cocking them and replacing the access panels. Note how the apparently large red gun patches are in fact the previously black painted undersides showing through the overpainted sky colour.

This unidentified Spitfire being rearmed is another one that has had the port wing repainted underneath from black to sky. A clue to this, apart from the patchiness of the finish is the lack of stencilling. The gun patches again appear to be black underneath rather than red.

Inset: A heavily stained and weathered 222 Squadron Spitfire with Sgt Ernest Scott alongside. The fuselage roundel in this case has had a thinner yellow ring applied to the outside, although it looks as if the groundcrew originally tried the full width one!

CANNONS & L1007

Spitfire L1007 (left) was the first to be experimentally fitted with two 20mm Hispano cannons in June 1939. It was then delivered to operational squadrons in Scotland for front line trials. Mainly flown by P/O 'Cannon' Proudman it shared in the destruction of a He111 on 13 January and also 22 February.

On 15 May 1940 it collided with another Spitfire on landing at Drem and caught fire. The burnt out wreckage can be seen on the left of the background photo and in the inset below left.

More cannon armed Spitfires were made, but after troublesome trials with 19 Squadron in the Battle of Britain, they were withdrawn from service. In the meantime a purposely designed 'b' wing was installed on MkI X4257 carrying two 20mm cannons and 4 .303 machine guns. This configuration proved successful and paved the way for the standard armament of most future Mks.

X4257 can be seen below, note the semi-recessed oil cooler, only seen on MkIs and MkIIs.

This rare press photo dated 7 August 1940 shows Czech groundcrew being lectured in front of a 19 Squadron Spitfire at Duxford. Of interest is the light coloured spinner tip which can also be seen in the only known photo of one of the squadron's cannon armed MkIbs (inset). These early Ibs didn't have machine guns in the outer wings so when the cannons jammed, as they frequently did, the pilot was effectively disarmed and had to withdraw from combat rapidly.

Spitfire P9386 was a temporary replacement for 19 Squadron's malfunctioning cannon armed Spitfires, arriving on 3 September from 7 OTU somewhat poorly maintained and 'smelling of vomit and sweat' according to the groundcrew.

There has been a lot of discussion about the colour of the spinner, with white or yellow being the most likely answers. The inset photo top right showing its pilot Brian Lane (second left) would suggest that the spinner is yellow.

Inset top left: An earlier QV-K showing a very different style of lettering for 19 Squadron.

SPITFIRE P9386 QV-K 19 SQUADRON

Modeller's notes

Aircraft:
Standard aerial with wire
Bulged cockpit canopy
Armoured windscreen
Standard pitot tube
Reflector gunsight
Standard DH prop and spinner
External rear view mirror

Colours:
'A' camouflage scheme
QV-K in light grey
Sky undersides, (no stencilling)
High demarcation line on nose
Red fabric gun patches.
Oversized fuselage roundel
Yellow spinner

Discussion points:
It's impossible to say whether
P9386 had gas patches on the
upper surfaces. George Unwin's
X4425 did (right), but others on the
squadron at the same time didn't.

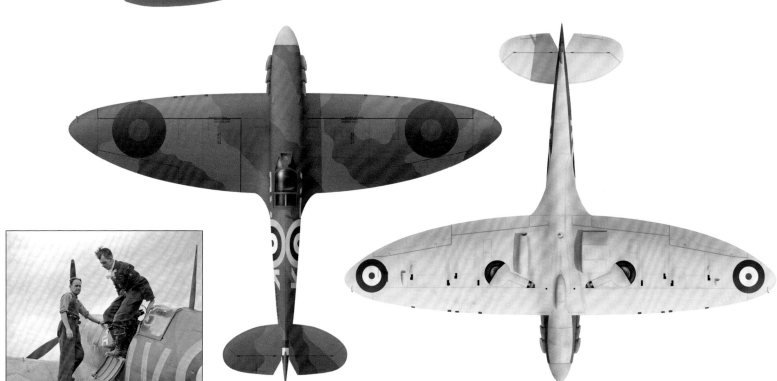

152 Squadron saw a lot of action in the south-west of England during the Battle.

Right: Sergeant Derek Robinson crash landed K9894 UM-N near Wareham, Dorset, on 8 August 1940. The replacement 'N' is seen below, note the huge letter size, seen on several 152 Sqn Spitfires in this period.

Bottom: Eric 'Boy' Marrs in the cockpit of 'Old Faithful' so named because it had amassed over 300 flying hours by the summer of 1940. Note that it even has the old door opening mechanism. Fortunately for Marrs it has been fitted with all the cockpit armour and even has a rear view mirror.

Two battle damaged Spitfires. In the background is L1082 of 609 Squadron which was damaged by Me110s over Ryde on 24 August 1940. The pilot, American Andy Mamedoff, is standing in the hole in his elevator!

Inset is P9391 another replacement delivered from 7 OTU to 19 Squadron on 3 September. Just two days later, a cannon shell blew away part of the fin, but 25-year-old Pilot Officer Eric Burgoyne, seen here, managed to return to Fowlmere. He was killed in action just three weeks later.

Both Spitfires have the serial number painted in small characters on the top of the fin and L1082 has what appears to be a small gas detection patch on the starboard tailplane.

Rearming and refuelling complete, one groundcrewman pulls the electric starter away whilst another waits on the wing to strap the pilot in. This 66 Squadron Spitfire LZ-N R6800 is said to have had a red spinner. The story goes that the C/O had misidentified his wingman on his tail during a combat and so ordered all his squadron aircraft to be painted with red spinners. It is also true that Fighter Command was experimenting with quick recognition features for its aircraft at the time so this may also be an explanation. A 501 Squadron Hurricane is just visible in the background, as is the Thames Estuary.

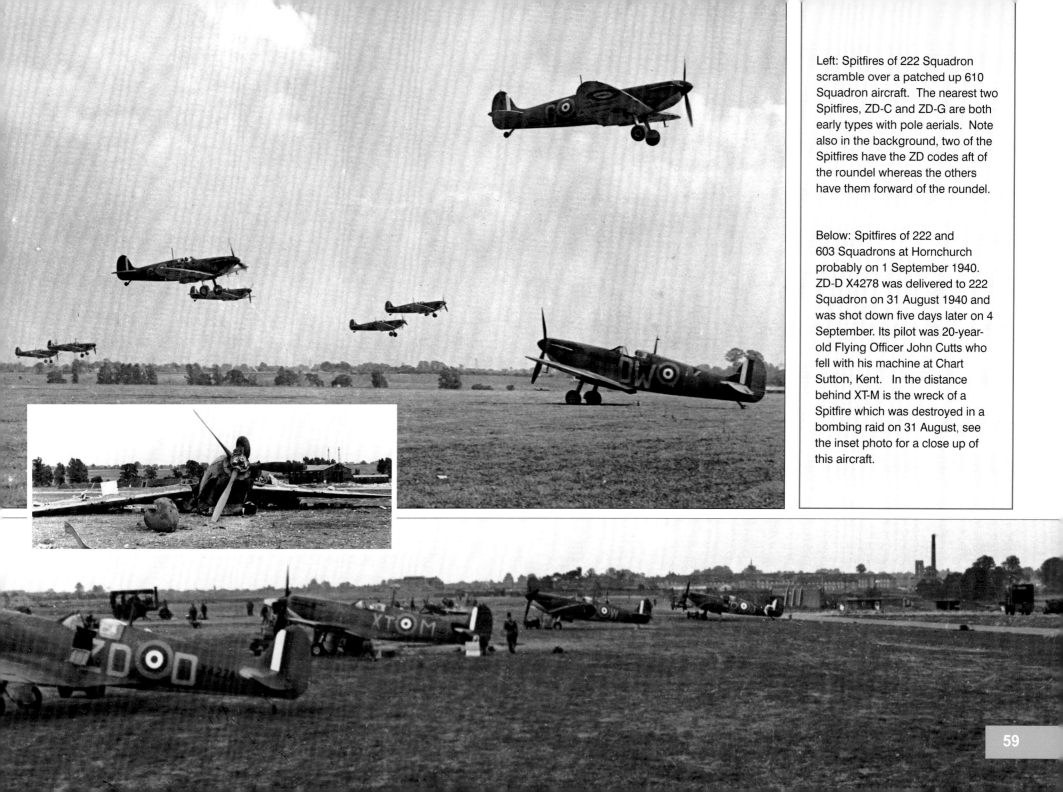

Left: Spitfires of 222 Squadron scramble over a patched up 610 Squadron aircraft. The nearest two Spitfires, ZD-C and ZD-G are both early types with pole aerials. Note also in the background, two of the Spitfires have the ZD codes aft of the roundel whereas the others have them forward of the roundel.

Below: Spitfires of 222 and 603 Squadrons at Hornchurch probably on 1 September 1940. ZD-D X4278 was delivered to 222 Squadron on 31 August 1940 and was shot down five days later on 4 September. Its pilot was 20-year-old Flying Officer John Cutts who fell with his machine at Chart Sutton, Kent. In the distance behind XT-M is the wreck of a Spitfire which was destroyed in a bombing raid on 31 August, see the inset photo for a close up of this aircraft.

The following five pages are from a press photo session taken at Fowlmere on 26 September 1940.

This Spitfire spent a month with 266 Squadron before being transferred to 616 Squadron. The UO codes have been modified into the QJ codes and the individual letter has been changed from a B or a P. It could be one of three Spitfires, X4172, X4174 or X4175. The flaking paint on the fin can be seen on several X serialled Spitfires around this time.

The same Spitfire minutes later being refuelled. Note the camera gun aperture in the port wing root. The Trolley Accumulator is plugged into the electrical socket just in front of the starboard wing root, ready to supply power to start the engine. This socket was removed on the MkII as the engine was started with a Coffman cartridge starter.

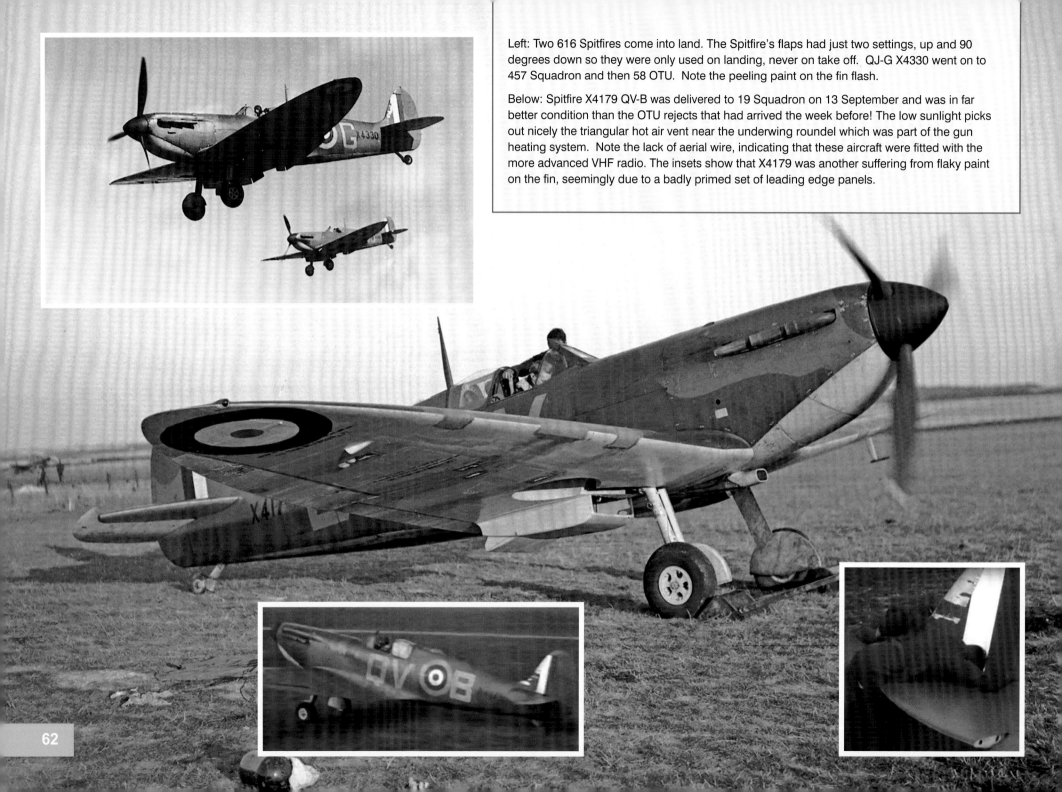

Left: Two 616 Spitfires come into land. The Spitfire's flaps had just two settings, up and 90 degrees down so they were only used on landing, never on take off. QJ-G X4330 went on to 457 Squadron and then 58 OTU. Note the peeling paint on the fin flash.

Below: Spitfire X4179 QV-B was delivered to 19 Squadron on 13 September and was in far better condition than the OTU rejects that had arrived the week before! The low sunlight picks out nicely the triangular hot air vent near the underwing roundel which was part of the gun heating system. Note the lack of aerial wire, indicating that these aircraft were fitted with the more advanced VHF radio. The insets show that X4179 was another suffering from flaky paint on the fin, seemingly due to a badly primed set of leading edge panels.

Left: The shape of thing to come. One of the interesting things captured by the press photographers on 26 September was this brand new Spitfire MkII which had just been delivered to 19 Squadron. Within two days, all the squadron's MkIs had been replaced by MkIIs.

Below: QV-I X4474 is guided by groundcrew to a parking area. The view over the nose of the Spitfire on the ground was terrible so groundcrew were frequently on hand to guide the pilots in. Note the very small underwing roundels on both X4474 and P7420. This is a sign that both aircraft were prepared for service at Number 6 Maintenance Unit (6MU). Each MU appears to have had its own preferences when it came to applying these roundels. X4179 (opposite page) came through 24MU which applied a slightly larger wingtip roundel.

Early evening of 26 September and 616 Squadron Spitfires leave Fowlmere, heading home to Kirton in Lindsey in Lincolnshire after spending the day operating with the Duxford Wing. The squadron did this journey every day from 20-28 September 1940 as part of a Big Wing tactical experiment. Note that all the Spitfires have the radiator flap fully open, essential when on the ground to stop the engine overheating.

The second aircraft in the lower photo, QJ-R X4328, was shot down the following day over Faversham, Kent. Pilot Officer Donald Smith died of his injuries shortly afterwards.

23-year-old Cyril Babbage from Ludlow in Shropshire had been shot down or damaged in combat three times already when on 12 October, his Spitfire X4541 was so badly damaged in combat that Cyril was forced to land at Iford Farm in West Sussex. LO-M overturned on landing, but the pilot escaped injury. Cyril continued to fly Spitfires until he was posted to a Mosquito squadron - when he was shot down twice more! He survived the war and died in 1976.

X4541 is another newly delivered aircraft from 24MU so has the slightly larger wingtip roundels. From the painter's point of view the wingtip roundels were clearly applied so as not to interfere with gun panels, stencilling or the pitot tube.

X4541 is also interesting as it has a 'wavy line' demarcation on the leading edge something only seen on 602 Squadron Spitfires.

609 Squadron groundcrew pose with PR-H towards the end of the Battle of Britain. The large letter painted under the nose was to help them see their aircraft after landing and guide them in.

PR-H is very unusual in that it has a PR style blister in the side of the canopy (arrowed).

The bulged blister in the side of the canopy was first used on Photo-reconnaissance Spitfires to help the pilot see the locations on the ground down and to the rear of the aircraft, which was the angle that the oblique camera was facing, as can be seen below on Spitfire X4786 a converted MkI.

The fact that both PR-H and PR-L, (pictured right), have this blistered canopy would suggest that either 609 was trialling them at the end of the Battle or that someone on the squadron had a mate on the PRU! This photo is also of interest because the Spitfire in the distance has the new 'skyband' painted around the rear fuselage which was introduced in November 1940, whereas PR-L is still in its Battle of Britain colours.

By the end of the Battle of Britain, many of the MkIs coming out of the factory were being painted as presentation aircraft. This was a result of the highly successful 'Spitfire Fund' project which invited communities and individuals to raise enough money to 'buy' a Spitfire for the RAF and have it named how they wished.

Left is 'Falkland Islands III' QJ-H in service with 92 Squadron. This aircraft was one of 10 Spitfires purchased by the Islanders. Its serial is a bit of a mystery as the records say that 'III' didn't fly with 92 Sqn but 'IV' did (X4616). However the aircraft in the photo has a painted out Z next to the roundel, (visible in other photos), so it must be X4614 which flew with 66 Squadron (LZ) before joining 92 Squadron.

Below is R7155 'Kikuyu-Embu, presented by native tribes in Kenya.

The MkIs were soon relegated to second line duties after the Battle of Britain with many new squadrons forming with them before quickly moving onto the later MkIIs and MkVs. The background photo shows a formation of MkIs of 457 Squadron out of Jurby on the Isle of Man.

Left: Spitfire X4244 GK-U of 52 OTU after being pranged by a student on 15 April 1942.

The unsung heroes of the Battle of Britain were the groundcrews who worked around the clock to keep the Spitfires serviceable. Here, a group of 222 Squadron groundcrew pose for a photo with one of their aircraft. The rear view mirror is just one of many styles seen during this period. Note that they are carefully keeping within the black walkway lines on the wing root.

Another point worth mentioning is that the MkI's cockpit door didn't have a crowbar attached, this was only added on later Mks.

And of course the Spitfire was nothing without the brave men who flew her into action. This is Leonard Haines of 19 Squadron posing for the Press on his Spitfire, note the simpler style of rear view mirror.

This angle shows well the shape of the MkI's 'kidney' exhausts.

THINGS YOU DON'T SEE ON A PRE 1941 MkI

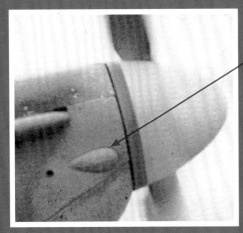

Coffman Starter bulge, introduced on the MkII to enable the pilot to start the engine without outside assistance.

Internal armoured windscreen, introduced 1941/42 on factory production lines.

Square glass reflector gunsight. This was introduced in 1941, all BofB period reflector gunsights were round.

Circular oil cooler. Again, another common mistake and again due to P7350 having this type of fitting. All 1940 MkIs and MkIIs had a semi recessed oil cooler. The full circle was introduced to give increased cooling power in 1941, mainly to the MkV.

Wing strengthening strakes. A common mistake made by artists depicting BofB Spitfires due to the BBMF Spitfire P7350 having them. In reality they were not introduced until 1942.

Crowbar in the door. Introduced from 1941 and never red in wartime!

Electrical socket in port wing root. This was on the other side in front of the wing on the MkI.